DAYS IN DEVONPORT
Part VI

Gerald W. Barker

Out muster?

It is difficult to tell whether the Dockyard workers are going in or leaving. The cycle shed was just inside the gates, and the bottom of Albert Road would be a seething mass of bicycles when the signal to stop work was given. Normans pianos are being advertised outside the small hut, where one could buy a newspaper.

This version of the book is virtually as originally published, presenting the work of Gerald W Barker. There are now additional pages at the back providing information about the publisher, Arthur L Clamp.

The republishing project is being managed by Arthur's grandson, Steven Gibson. We aim to find all the research that he was involved in publishing, preserving it for the next generation as part of 'The Clamp Collection'.

Introduction

Among those who were born in or near what was once known as the *Three Towns*, Devonport was well represented by those men and women who brought lustre to the area. Some of the following were born in Devonport:

Sir John Hawkins: 1532-1595. Many historians believed him to be the father of the Royal Navy. He was 3rd in command during the Battle of the Armada.

Captain Robert Falcon Scott, R.N.: 1868-1912. Great Explorer of the Antarctic. He reached the Pole 18th January, 1912. Shortly after Roald Amundsen's Norwegian expedition.

Captain Tobias Furneaux: The first man to circumnavigate the world in both directions 1766-8 and 1772-4. He was christened at Stoke Damerel Church.

Sir Charles Lock Eastlake: painted the historical picture of Napoleon on H.M.S. *Bellerophon* in Plymouth Sound.

Benjamin Haydon: painted *The Raising of Lazarus*.

Solomon Hart: painted *The Execution of Lady Jane Grey*.

Samuel Prout: was one of the greatest artists of picturesque England.

Sir Joshua Reynolds: Celebrated painter. First President of the Royal Academy.

N. T. Carrington: The Dartmoor poet, and schoolteacher. From 1809-1839 he carried on his "ACADEMY" near Morice Square.

Reverend R. S. Hawker: One of the most popular amongst Westcountry authors.

Professor Robert Hunt: Eminent Geologist. Took a leading part in the educational work of the Devonport Mechanics Institute.

Professor J. C. Adams: Astronomer and discoverer of the planet *Neptune*.

Sir William White: Chief Constructor of the Queen's Navy.

Edward Stanley Gibbons: Philatelist. Founder of the famous firm of stamp dealers.

Doctor Mabel Ramsey: Pioneering woman surgeon 1st October, 1900. Entered Edinburgh University as a medical student.

Wayne Sleep: Rose from the ranks of the Royal Ballet to become one of the country's top dancing personalities. Named Showbusiness Personality by the Variety Club of Great Britain when the 1983 awards were presented.

Samuel Phelps: Born 1804. Became a famous actor in 1844 and manager of the Sadlers Wells Theatre giving the theatre such a high standard of excellence that it rivalled Covent Garden.

Maria Foote: (later Countess of Harrington) took London by storm when she appeared at Covent Garden in 1814. Her father was once manager of the Royal Theatre.

Angela Rippon: Became the first woman B.B.C. Television Newsreader.

Ron Goodwin: Musical Composer, *633 Squadron, Battle of Britain, Those Magnificent Men in their Flying Machines*.

Donald Sinden: Named in 1977 as the "Actor of the Year" Awarded C.B.E.

Frederick Harvey: His Master's Voice Company (1948) was given the accolade of being one of the finest baritones singing in Great Britain.

Sharon Davies: Olympic Swimmer. Winner of the Sports Writers and Sportswoman of the Year Award. At 15 she won a record of seven National Titles. She won a silver medal at the Moscow Olympics, 1980.

David Webb: Broke the international canoeing record with a world beating 2500 miles paddle from the arctic ice to Bergen in Norway.

Trevor Francis: England's first million pounds transfer footballer

Tony Willis: Despite having a leg amputated became a teacher of physical education and in the 1980 Olympic Games for the Disabled won a silver and gold medal for Great Britain.

Rt. Hon. Michael Foot: President of the Council. Leader of the Labour Party. Freeman of the City.

Rt. Hon. David Owen: Labour, Navy Minister, Health Minister, Foreign Secretary when 38, leader of the Social Democratic Party.

Leslie Hore-Belisha: Liberal National 1923. Secretary of State for War in 1939.

Major Edmund Lockyer: born 1784. Founded the first British Settlement in Western Australia.

Dame Jocelyn Woollcombe: C.B.E., former Director, W.R.N.S.

Lieutenant John Chard: V.C. Commander of the tiny force that on 22nd January, 1879, held the mission station of Rorke's Drift on Buffalo river on the border between Natal and Zululand against more than 3000 Zulu warriors.

Major Sir A. H. S. Waters: V.C., C.B.E., D.S.O., M.C. World War I. Awarded the V.C. during the last week of the war for completing a bridge in France while under heavy fire which had killed all his officers and N.C.Os.

Captain Frederick John Walker: C.B., D.S.O. and three bars (1896-1944). According to an Admiralty statement: "Did more to free the Atlantic of the U boat menace than any other single officer". He died in 1944 owing to "War Weariness". He was the Senior Officer of the famous Second Escort Group.

Lieutenant Philip Curtis: V.C., aged 24. When severely injured continued to charge the enemy until dead. Battle of the Injun River Korea, 1951.

Acknowledgements

He has never been to the South Pole and, to my knowledge, has had no leaning towards the stage, but, nevertheless, deserves to be mentioned on this page if only for the fact that Arthur L. Clamp has been involved in the publication of over forty such local publications as *Days in Devonport*. Thanks also to Mr. F. E. Pine, Administrator of Devonport Hospital, and Mr. L. Presland, X-Ray Department of Derriford Hospital, for their continued help with Devonport Hospital material. Also to Mr. S. P. Greenwood, Mr. H. H. Greenwood, Mr. R. Rundell, Secretary of the Hertfordshire Postcard Club, Mr. G. Fleming, Mrs. M. Godden, Mr. J. Williams, Mr. D. G. Furnace, Mr. R. Blagdon, Mr. R. Smith, Mrs. E. Miller, Mrs. M. Trethowen, Mr. G. Piper, Mrs. B. Hearn, Mrs. M. Laxton, Mrs. B. Elliot, Mr. R. Glover, Mrs. J. R. Gribbell, Mrs. L. M. Hooper, Mr. J. Blazier, Mr. H. Feabes, Mr. R. W. Ellery, Mrs. F. McTighe, Miss S. Barker, Mr. L. R. Bromley, Mrs. M. Bonning, Mr. J. Prance, Mr. C. Symons, Mr. C. F. J. Soulsby, Mr. P. F. Ghillyer, Mrs. C. Gardner and Mr. E. Yeo.

Gerald Barker,
44, Burnham Park Road,
Peverell, Plymouth

The Hospital on the Hill

The Devonport Section of the Plymouth General Hospital, as the Royal Albert Hospital became known in 1963. The balcony underneath the triangular shaped top part, in the front of the building, was demolished in the 1960s. The rectangular structure stands in front of the main entrance door where the inscription on the wall read:
"ROYAL ALBERT HOSPITAL AND EYE INFIRMARY SUPPORTED BY VOLUNTARY CONTRIBUTIONS. ESTABLISHED 1861".

This plaque was situated in Norman Ward (Men's Ward).

List of Presidents of the Royal Albert Hospital

The first President of the new Hospital was Major General W. N. Hutchinson, Lieutenant Governor of Plymouth, and amongst the first Life Governors. The Prince of Wales (afterwards King Edward VII). The Earl Fortescue. The Earls of Mount Edgcumbe and St. Germans. Lord Clinton. T. J. Agar Roberts, Esq., M. P. Edward St. Aubyn, Esq., N.B. William Henry, the 4th Earl of Mount Edgcumbe, was President in the years 1869–70 and 1876–77. No less than 26 of the 63 Presidents who were elected during the period 1863–1934 were directly connected with either the navy or army.

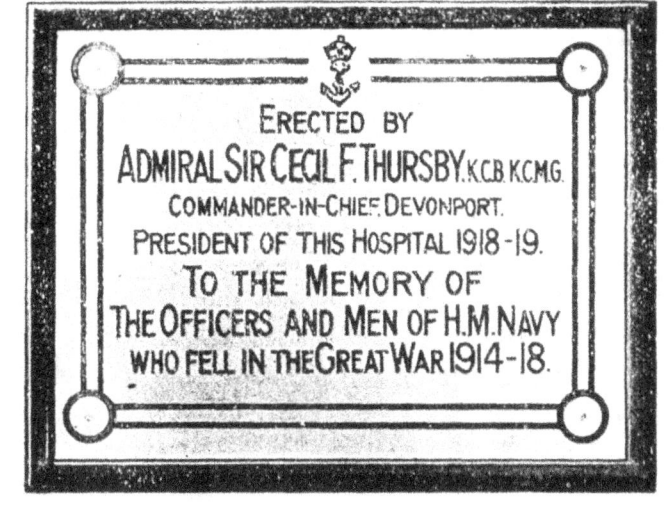

They Also Serve

Civilians and servicemen gave a great deal of voluntary service to the hospital by serving on various committees. Those sitting outside the main kitchen, below the gold leaf lettering at the top of the building reading:
"ROYAL ALBERT HOSPITAL SUPPORTED BY VOLUNTARY CONTRIBUTIONS",
included Mr. George Wherry, 2nd from left, A. W. Grigg, A. J. M. Venning and Mrs. E. J. Perkins. The time is believed to be in the 1920s.

1931 Fête

A group of voluntary workers in the hospital grounds on the occasion of a Fête organised by Devonport Royal Albert Hospital Entertainments Committee in 1931. *Back row*: F. C. Godfree, M. Clift, R. Mitchelmore, D. G. Evans, F. Rowe *Centre*: R. Roper, S. Tremaine, F. E. Pine, R. Chudley, W. Lewis, E. Pearce, H. E. Sainbell *Front row*: Mrs. E. J. Perkins, A. Down, K. Eyton Peck, R. C. Ward and J. A. Cusack.

List of Wards of Royal Albert Hospital

Harry Wright Ward, Sir, J.P., former Lord Mayor.
Washbourne Ward, Percy, former Lord Mayor
Charles Lander Ward, Hon. Surgeon. D.S.O., M.C., J.P., City Councillor
Mayhew Ward, M.D., M.A.
Norman Ward, after Architect's wife.
Adams Ward, after Mrs. Adams, generous benefactor.
Emma Ward, Lady Templeton. former Children's Ward, Lady St. Aubyn.

Going Down, 1983

One of the concerns of some citizens was that the demolition of the Devonport Hospital was carried out before April or failing this after August, as a small colony of housemartins made their nests in the crevices in the stonework each spring, attempting to raise their brood after a flight of some 7,000 hazardous miles to this building, which was their summer home.   4C

Now Wash Your Hands

In the 1920s inside the children's ward was a basin and jug that stood on a table. This was for the doctors and surgeons to wash their hands. The lovely stained glass window was destroyed when it was blown out by bomb blast during the air raids in the Second World War. The author remembers, as a youth, breaking his arm playing football and walking from Central Park, during an air raid, to the Casualty Department of the hospital to have it attended.

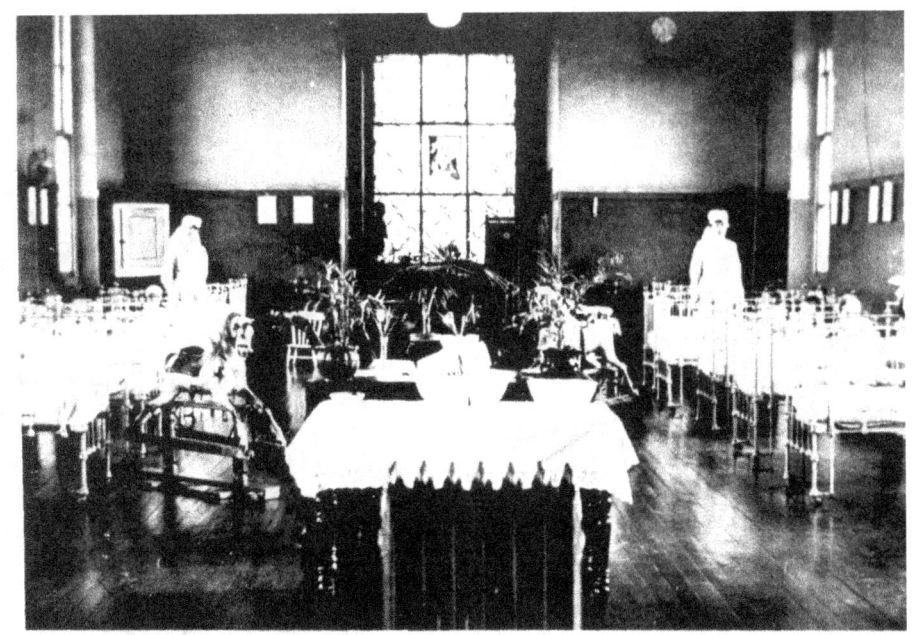

Operating Theatre, 1908

One of the many nurses who gave dedicated service to Devonport Hospital was Sister Jane Lilley, who is standing left foreground. She was then aged twenty-four.

Outside the Nurses Home, 1932

H.R.H. The Princess Henry of Battenburg, a Patron of the Hospital, laid the foundation stone of the Nurses' Home on 9th June, 1899. In the group are: Mrs. F. H. Dorrell, Masseuse, Sisters N. G. Paget, M. Forsythe, D. Stacey, I. Lamont, E. C. Pratt and M. A. Rice.

Cavalry Advance!

Not when this photograph was taken, but earlier in the time of the Crimean War. The occasion, however, was a friendly one. The Hussar cavalry made such a splendid sight that they were asked by the citizens to specially parade through Fore Street en route to embarkation in the dockyard. In the 1850s the Hussar Regiment, in full dress, gave a dazzling display and were hailed by the admiring crowds as they rode through the Dockyard Gates.

Church Parade, 1912

The National Reserve Church Parade 8th December, 1912, marching from Fore Street down Catherine Street. The advertisements on the walls tell the locals that Sally Bishop from the *Prince of Wales* Theatre in London is coming to the *Grand Theatre* in Union Street. J. B. Love's Emporium is half way up on the left. The parade could be on its way to the church in James Street or on its way to the Devonport Guildhall.

Exmouth Hall

The Devonport Park War Memorial is to be seen in front of the horse and cart. The hoarding on the left of the cart is advertising *Norman and Son's Pianos*. The Devonport Great Western Railway Station was on the left. If one was standing outside the Exmouth Hall large white letters on the wall above the nearby G.W.R. Station read: *Devonport High School for Boys*. It was painted out in 1939 so that in the event of invasion the enemy would not be helped.

Brass Cannon

This stood at the eastern end of Mount Wise Parade. It was captured from the Turks in the Dardanelles. Admiral Sir J. T. Duckworth brought the cannon back from the Dardanelles in 1807. It was mounted on an elegant iron carriage cast for the purpose with appropriate ornaments and inscriptions. The date of the photograph is probably the late 1920s.

The Parade, Mount Wise

When the troops of the Garrison were mustered to celebrate some national event Mount Wise presented a joyous scene. Thousands of happy smiling faces would enjoy the beautiful scenery. The batteries of Mount Wise overlooked the fine bay, the Sound, with the Breakwater, heights of Staddon and ships-of-war lying at their anchors with lovely Mount Edgcumbe behind them. At the summit of the hill is the semaphore where all signals were made with the Admiral of ships that were passing up and down the channel within sight of the coast.

Devonport High School for Boys (Rear View)

This building was originally erected as a High School for Girls by the Plymouth Stonehouse and District High Schools Company in 1878. It was purchased by the Devonport Corporation in September, 1906. Formerly occupied by the Devonport, Stoke and Stonehouse High School for Girls, it became recognised as a fully equipped Secondary School for Boys. Fees were charged for some pupils until the passing of the 1944 Education Act. The building (still standing in Albert Road) was conveniently situated close to the G.W.R. Station.

Morice Square

Decorations enhance the pleasant surroundings. Many Devonport people remember sitting among the leafy trees with the stately spire of St. Paul's Church across the cobbled street. Excited children would make their way past the circular green towards Cornwall Street en route to North Corner to catch the ferry to Cornwall.

Co-operative Tea Specialists

The date of the carnival is 16th July, 1927. The float with its shades is passing between the Brickfields and Bluff Battery. Someone has left their motor bike, perhaps to get a view of the procession. The bike is stationed approximately at the foot of steps (still to be seen) leading to the summit of the Battery.

First Prize

A notice is proudly displayed declaring the winning of first prize in the Carnival. The striped pole in the window of the shoe repairer, "Phillips Soles" High Class Repairs, helps to supplement the decorations. The four wheels on the pram probably were destined to become part of a trolley. This form of transport, with youngsters skilfully steering around obstacles, was to be seen and used by the author in many streets during the 1930's.

"To Let"

So reads the notice at the back of the lorry in the carnival procession of 1927. On the side of the card reads, "Particulars from Frank Pearson of 9, Whimple Street". In less happier times, during the early 1940s, a steel-domed machine gun-post was situated on the grass where the people are watching the procession pass. It stood ready to guard Stonehouse Bridge a few yards down the road. Ron Smith and the author remember, as boys, playing inside it, once the danger of invasion had passed.

Heading for Stonehouse Bridge

Arctic is the bold lettering on this van as it heads for Stonehouse in the 1927 carnival. A bear's head can be seen on the bottom of the picture to the left of the man. This part of the Brickfields, during the war of 1939, became an area of slit trenches. Mr. R. Smith remembers seeing the searchlight battery and anti-Aircraft battery in the vicinity. The lower part of the slopes, facing Kings Road, were eventually used for the building of pre-fabs.

Bass in Bottle

This shows Ash and Sons "float" outside the canteen of South Raglan Barracks. They are the winners of the first prize. Some of the names remembered were:
On the left: Mr. Field, Mr. Hawkin, Mr. Hayes, Mr. Flynn.
On the right: Mr. Barter, Mr. Clark, who was the boss, and Mr. Taylor the foreman.

St. Joseph's School, Mutton Cove, 1932

The Junior mixed class of eight year olds at St. Joseph's Roman Catholic School. The boys and girls of Standard II were: Ronald Murphy, William Cremin, Francis Northcote, Stanley Hole, Jack Hove, Desmond Furnace, Thomas Silcox, Shaun Donovan, Francis Taylor Lawrence Griffin, Patricia Cavanagh, Mary Griffin, Doreen Ashton, Maleta Vassallo, Patricia Campbell, Joan Merriell and Josephine Fitzgerald. The rooms of the school remain on the site adjacent to "Knights" Store.

Maypole Dancing, 1925

At No. 3 Mutton Cove dancing around the maypole was practised in the garden that was common to five homes. On the big day itself it was danced in the middle of the quay between the railings and the Green. A slippery pole would also be to hand with a big pig's head on the end with a flag in its mouth. The man who got the flag got the head!

Devonport to Gibraltar, 1914–1918

"I agree to submit myself to navy discipline and to allow myself to be trained in the use of guns and firearms to defend Gibraltar in the event of invasion". This is one of the clauses in Mr. H. H. Greenwood's father's contract who was appointed to the Gibraltar shipyards in 1907. For the sum of just over what today would be nearly £2 a week plus a foreign service allowance of 75p, Mr. Thomas Greenwood was sent overseas for one year with the possibility of a further two years in Gibraltar added to the contract.

The Marvellous "Toy"

Together with his Devonport friends, the author would catch a train to Millbay railway station opposite the Duke of Cornwall Hotel. After a short stop to climb over the First World War tank, (later to be melted down to help the War effort in the 1940's, the plinth is still to be seen in Millbay Park) they would make their way to the Ballard's Institute, a few yards away in the vicinity where Telecom now stands. Many boys enjoyed the club, built by Mr. A. C. Ballard, the philanthropist, who cared for the welfare of boys.

The Torpoint Ferry

One of the old ferries had a large number of bulls and cows in transport when some of them escaped off the prow just before reaching the Devonport end. They swam around for ages before being rounded up. The author remembers seeing the Devonport-built and Devonport-manned H.M.S. *Exeter* passing. He was standing on the Devonport side of the ferry in February 1940. The cruiser had been battered in the sinking of the *Graf Spee*. Mr. Winston Churchill, the First Lord of the Admiralty, was on hand to do honour to the brave ship's company.

J. HEALY & SON,
Builders & Undertakers,
33, PRINCES STREET, DEVONPORT.

REPAIRS IN MASONS', CARPENTERS', & JOINERS' WORK.

Funerals Furnished.

VENETIAN BLINDS Made to Order.

ALL ORDERS PROMPTLY ATTENDED TO.

Vehicles of Beauty

All the harnesses of the horses looked beautiful. The black leathers were always shining as new and the brasses on the harnesses gleamed. Many Devonport people remember the later vehicles of Sibley's of Mutton Cove. It was a real sight to see for onlookers such as Mr. Pat Ghillyer, when a boy. They owned the finest crystal funeral hearses in the Westcountry. The drivers always wore the breeches with polished black leggings lined inside with white. The coach drivers wore top hats. All horses during funerals wore the cockade in their headgear. These were much in evidence in the 1920's.

Len Harvey

He was aged fifteen when the photograph was taken. A plaque in honour of their famous pupil was erected in York Street School. Mr. Pat Ghillyer, who now lives in Crownhill, remembers chasing this one-time puny lad through one end of Jimmy Love's Emporium in Catherine Street and out the other end. Len Harvey's father, at the Devonia Boxing Club, would give a massage for sixpence (6d.) and the boxers would feel "over the moon".

Bugler Lake

He lived in Monument Street, Devonport. In 1923 he won the British and European bantam-weight title Mr. Ernie Drake remembers the Devonport Boxing Club which in 1921 was situated near the Customs House in North Corner. Cartlidge also trained here. He was a Royal Naval boxer and at that time they had no comparable facilities of their own. The club was run by Johnny Williams, the trainer

Boxing Finalists, 1945

Many Devonport boys "sailed away" on the Torpoint Ferry to join the Royal Naval Artificer Apprentices in H.M.S. Fisgard (closed 1983). Formerly they were billeted in St. Mark's Hall, Ford, Devonport in 1939, and later in the vacated Stoke Damerel High School for Girls, Keppel Place, Devonport. The author is standing extreme right with other members of the boxing team in front of the factory clock. The apprentices were trained by champion boxer Seaman Tommy Watson, and Paddy Brown who played centre-forward for Plymouth Argyle in the 1940s. They were R.N. Physical Training Instructors.

Police Inspector

Mr. James Willcocks was a police inspector in the Devonport Borough Police Force. He inaugurated the Police Sick Mutual Fund at Devonport and took a keen interest in organising concerts and river trips for the benefit of local charities. He retired in 1912, having served under Chief Constables Lynn, Evans, Matters and Watson. At his funeral in 1925 the pall-bearers were brother officers Det. Inspector S. Lucas, Inspectors G. Warwick, R. Pryor, Joseph Voss, J. Gulley and J. T. Way.

The Alhambra Theatre

The *Alhambra*, which opened in 1924, was advertised as the "Family Resort". It was a focal point of entertainment in the thriving Devonport of the 1930's. It was billed as having a continuous performance. First known as the *Empire Theatre* in 1895 and then a year or so later as the *Metropole* until 1914. It was blitzed on 23rd April, 1941. It stood at the junction of York Street (previously known as Cherry Garden Street) and Tavistock Street. This was a very busy street with Devonport Market and the large shop of Boolds, plus many smaller shops.

Tavistock Street

The *Metropole* stands on the right hand side at the top of the street. At the matinees on Saturdays it would cost 2d. (approx one penny) for a two-hour play. Some of the dramas remembered were: *Maria Marten* or *The Murder in the Red Barn* and *East Lynne*. The closing years of the last century witnessed a notable theatrical revival in the opening of the *Metropole Theatre*. The entertainment seemed to revive the traditions of the Old Dock Theatre. Vociferous audiences were composed largely of sailors who took the heroines to their hearts, reviled the villains, and cheered the gallant heroes to the echo.

I Remember
Marjorie Claxton

I remember Devonport, Stonehouse and Plymouth when they were three separate boroughs each thriving independently in their own particular way.

It was a pleasant walk from Devonport to Plymouth via Stonehouse. Transport was mainly by trams, which ran from the terminus in Fore Street, Devonport, down Chapel Street, stopping at Cumberland Gardens to pick up passengers, then on along past the Raglan Barracks on the left and Mt. Wise on the right then down over the hill past the Brickfields, crossing Kings Road and on over the Stoneferry Bridge, through the toll gate commonly known as the *Halfpenny Gate*. Here one was in Stonehouse where the trams stopped in Edgcumbe Street to pick up folk. The route continued through Union Street passing several Theatres and cinemas such as the *Grand*, the *Palace*, the *Savoy* and the *Gaiety*, on to Derry's clock, the Plymouth terminus. I remember the fascination of watching the conductor changing the trolley arm over onto the other overhead wire for the return journey. If the conductor happened to be short, this task could be tricky, as the arm was heavy and would swing and spark until it eventually clicked on the wire.

Underneath the halfpenny gate bridge was Stonehouse Creek, and at high tide the stream reached as far as the Military Hospital Boys from High Street, had fine fun challenging each other to ride the logs. These huge logs, chained together, belonged to Fox Elliot the timber merchants and were towed up the creek by boat and left there to season. On the other side of the bridge, underneath it, were several boathouses approached from Richmond Walk side of Kings Road. My uncle and aunt had a motor boat and used to take me with them on trips to Barn Pool, Cawsand, and sometimes to picnic on the breakwater. I learned to row a boat on Stonehouse Creek, mainly because my boy cousins used to tease me and I wanted to do as well as they.

I remember vividly the day I went to visit my aunt and uncle in Stonehouse. Being a lovely summer day, I felt quite important at being allowed to go alone at eight years of age. My home was at the Mt. Wise end of George Street, Devonport, so I walked up through the beautiful Mt. Wise Avenue, stopping for a few minutes to watch the naval officers playing cricket, then turned right past the ramparts and the New Cut leading to Richmond Walk, then on down over the hill across Kings Road and to the toll gate. On production of a halfpenny I was allowed through the turnstiles having been issued with a return ticket.

It so happened my folks were going to visit friends so after about an hour, having had some lemonade and biscuits, I made my way back up over the bridge to the toll gate. Putting my hand in my pocket for my ticket I was horrified to find I'd lost it, and as the lady in charge was not the same one I saw before, she would not let me go through. Strangely enough the only other people around seemed to pass by in the tram or on bikes or horses and carts, so I was forced to turn back. However, I had an idea and went back, down by the brewery to the slip, hoping I might see somebody in the boathouses or even find a boat there in which case I could row across, but alas, no people about and no boat. Then I knew the only way I could get home was a long way around, so I went along High Street, along by the Naval Hospital wall, which seemed endless, and turned up into Eldad Hill, to make my way down to Millbridge. Then the bottom simply dropped out of my world, for there at the bottom of the hill facing me was another toll gate. This was just too much. I was panic stricken whereon the floodgates burst and I remember saying "Whatever shall I do?" between my sobs. Then a kindly voice said "What's the matter? Why are you crying like this?" looking up I had a blurred vision of a young soldier, who dried my tears as I had lost my handkerchief. He had a lovely face, so I blurted out my tale of woe, then he caught hold of my hand, escorted me through the gate and after asking where I lived and if I knew my way home, he gave me a penny and went on his way. I thanked him and ran through Fellows Place, up over Stoke Church Hill, past the Military Hospital. Then I came to a narrow road running between the Albion football ground and the Devonport South Western Station yard and the railway. There had recently been talk of a murder here, so being not only tired, but terrified, I took to my heels as if the very devil himself was after me. Out through the Rectory across Kings Road, on up over the Brickfields, down through Mt. Wise Avenue and eventually home.

More tears were shed then from sheer exhaustion and relief at being safely back with my mother. I remember the look of sheer amazement on her face, as she held me close while I poured out my story. Softly she told me she hoped I had learned to be more careful as I had lost my handkerchief as well as my ticket. When I gave her the penny she handed it back to me telling me to keep it as it was dated 1905 the year I was born.

Several years later I went to join a friendly society, and remember the surprise I had when the gentleman who opened the door, took my name and address, then said, "Aren't you the young lady who lost her toll gate ticket?" Then I remembered his face and after the meeting he escorted me home, met my mother, and became a close friend of the family. His young friend later became my dear husband for thirty years, during which time my children always knew my soldier friend as uncle. Both soldier and husband have passed on but I remember a lifetime of happiness and friendship brought about by the loss of a halfpenny toll gate ticket. By the way I still have that 1905 penny!

Halfpenny Bridge, Devonport

Dr. to F. Potter and Son

The Devonia Boxing Club had its premises finally over Potters in Mount Street. Before this it was situated in York Street above Ley's billiard hall. Prior to this, about 1938, it was above Ernie Drake's shop in Devonport Market. Boxing matches were held upstairs on Friday evenings. Mr. Drake remembers the 42 steps from the bottom to the next floor.

Pub Outing

Standing outside the *Post Office Inn*, 20 Market Street, Devonport, is Mr. Fred C. Potter, the well known Devonport Undertaker. He stands wearing a trilby and raincoat with his hands in his pockets. The pub outing was arranged by the proprietors, Mr. and Mrs. Eric. C. Potter (standing together at the right of picture). Mr. Bill C. Potter is looking over a woman's shoulder. *Right*. Market Street was adjacent to Devonport Market and lay between Cherry Gardens (later York Street) and Barrack Street. The whole Potter family was very well known to Devonport residents.

A Soldier's Thoughts

Captain Ernest Bradley remembered arriving in Devonport to join Raglan Barracks when serving with the South Wales Borderers in 1923. After leaving the King's Road Station (now the site of the College of Further Education) his first impression was of the beauty of the gardens in Devonport Park with its lovely display of flowers. He recalls the troops dry canteen situated on one side of the large main gate. Over this was the Head Office.

Destination India

26th September, 1911. The 1st Leinster Regiment is getting ready for transport to India. The writing on the back of the postcard reads. "Dear Mother and Father. In receipt of letter this morning. We do not go aboard now until Friday 3.30 p.m., and leave on Saturday. I will try to drop a line on the way. I remain your loving son, Bill." The troops quarters were on the west of the barracks (left in photo) and the Officer's quarters of the North Raglan Barracks were to the right of them.

Ten Smart Soldiers

A troupe of Geraldine Lamb's dancers who appeared at various times and places to give concerts to aid charity are seen in York Street (at the back of the present Devonport Central Hall, in Fore Street) at the rear of the *Tivoli* Cinema, probably in the late 1930's. The cast-iron structure in the right hand top of the picture was a men's toilet. At one time these were quite numerous.

Fore Street

The horse-drawn cab is parked in the vicinity of the present Devonport Methodist Central Hall. An electric tram is approaching the "Loop" in its track where another tram was allowed to pass it going in the opposite direction. The building on the right was at one time the Temperance Hall, built in 1850, becoming a Public Hall a few years later. Mr. Arthur Richard remembers standing in the side balcony singing with other lads, *Row for the Shore*. Mr. Coombes, Optician, was one of the first to put on a magic lantern slide show. It became the *Electric* Cinema in 1910.

Dockyard Gates 1918

Fore Street, one of the best looking streets in the city, culminated in the magnificent gateway of the South Yard. The night that the war broke out Ivy Ghillyer, now Mrs. Watson, remembers being kept awake all night listening to the mules bringing the guns out of the dockyard. She saw the wounded being brought back from the Somme. With other girls she gave concerts to raise money for the War effort. With victory in 1918 the Fore Street Dockyard Gates were floodlit.

Nissen Huts

The huts are situated on the site where the Royal Sailors' Rest stood in Fore Street in the heart of busy Devonport. In the 1940s coloured American troops lived in these huts that stretched right down Catherine Street. Barclay's Bank is on the corner of King Street. Some Devonport people remember the big band concerts held by the United States Forces in Fore Street.

Down by the Beacon

A new promenade, "Richmond Walk," was planned and constructed in 1809 by the Earl of Richmond, to allay discontent when access to the outer "lines" had been denied to the locals through the construction of an inner boundary wall towards the end of the century. Enjoying this access to the waterside is a small group taking a stroll. Bromley Cottages were demolished in 1953. Nos. 1 and 1a Richmond Walk were to the left of the Admiral's Steps. No. 2 Rose Cottage is still in existence and is now the home of the Blagdon family.

The Boat House, 1920s

Seen in the centre of the photo, the boat house had pulleys so that boats could be suspended above the water level. it had a floor about mid-way. To the right changing rooms for men bathers existed. Two flights of steps ran down from Richmond Walk to give access to the slabs for sunbathing. The sewerage pipe (foreground) has been cemented over to form bathing (landing) stages, giving walkers access to the sea.

Male Bathing Pool, about 1920

Known as "Pikey's", one of the flights of steps seen in the above picture led down to the "old swimming bath". A man on the right standing on the wall is giving instructions to boys that are secured to a rope. The high sea wall kept out any rubbish. Victoria Cottages, seen at the back, were adjacent to the site where the Royal Clarence Baths once stood. Mrs. L. Hooper, in book IV on page 20, is seen walking down the narrow path (still existing) that was behind the site of the cottages.

Passed by Censor

So reads the back of the card on which the Royal Naval Barracks is depicted. Also mentioned is Swiss and Sons, The Bookstall. The postmark was dated 1944 and the message read: "Have been in to Devonport this morning. It is a mess. Love, Nell." Passengers passing by on the top deck of a no. 7 or 14 bus would have had a good view of the motor cars just inside the wall.

The Park Pavilion

Behind the H.M.S. *Doris* gun stands the Park Pavilion where one could have refreshments such as teas, minerals and home-made ices. Devonport's coat of arms can be seen in the front of the building. The park-keeper, Mr. Baker, had his residence in the building. He was very strict and well respected by the boys and girls who played in the park. The wall to the rear of the gun stood on the northern perimeter of Granby Army Barracks.

Royal Naval Barracks Gymnasium

Fitness is one of the aims of making a naval rating efficient in his exacting job at sea. Whether it was the routine sword drill carried out on the ships of sail or the field gun crew training of more recent times, the athletic prowess of the individual was encouraged. To take part in the most hazardous of pursuits, that of taking a gun across a "chasm", and re-assembling it across the other side to fire it, needs a great deal of physical skill and courage.

The Old Chapel

This quaint old building at the corner of Duke and George Street, Devonport, was originally built for the Unitarians in the year 1790. The congregation of the chapel dwindled as it was understood that Commissioner Fanshaw intimated that all Dockyardsmen who attended the new chapel would be discharged as disloyal subjects. The French Revolution was then in full operation and it was believed at that time that the Unitarians were ardent supporters of it.

THIS quaint old building situate at the corner of Duke and George Streets Devonport, was originally built for the Unitarians in the year A.D. 1790. The Congregation of the Chapel decayed in consequence of its being understood that Commissioner Fanshaw intimated that all Dockyardsmen who attended the New Chapel would be discharged as disloyal subjects; the French Revolution was then in full operation, and the Unitarians were the most ardent admirers of that movement in Great Britain. Three of that sect were executed as ringleaders in a most disgraceful riot in Birmingham on the 14th July, 1791. Ten years afterwards, in 1801, the Chapel was converted, the conversion being as wide apart from its original purpose as could be imagined. The Chapel became a Temple of Bacchus, dedicated to the sale of Wines and Spirits, thus the change from Spiritual to the Spirituous. The old building still retains remnants of its ecclesiastical character, and a Chaplain is still attached, who performs certain duties with zeal and punctuality.

Interior of the Chapel

Three Unitarians were executed as ringleaders in a riot in Birmingham on 14th July, 1791. Ten years afterwards in 1801 the Chapel was converted, the conversion being wide apart from its original purpose. It became used for the sale of wines and spirits. The building retained remnants of its ecclesiastical character.

THIS quaint old building situate at the corner of Duke and George Streets, Devonport, was originally built for the Unitarians in the year A.D. 1790. The Congregation of the Chapel decayed in consequence of its being understood that Commissioner Fanshaw intimated that all Dockyardsmen who attended the New Chapel would be discharged as disloyal subjects; the French Revolution was then in full operation, and the Unitarians were the most ardent admirers of that movement in Great Britain. Three of that sect were executed as ringleaders in a most disgraceful riot in Birmingham on the 14th July, 1791. Ten years afterwards, in 1801, the Chapel was converted, the conversion being as wide apart from its original purpose as could be imagined. The Chapel became a Temple of Bacchus, dedicated to the sale of Wines and Spirits, thus the change from Spiritual to the Spirituous. The old building still retains remnants of its ecclesiastical character, and a Chaplain is still attached, who performs certain duties with zeal and punctuality.

The Old Gibbet

The gibbet stood opposite Stoke Church (Stoke Damerel) until 1827 when it was taken down. John Richards and William Smith were executed for the murder of Mr. Philip Smith, a clerk in the Dockyard in 1787. After execution their bodies were brought to Stoke where they were gibbeted. John Smith's body remained there for about seven years. The road went up past the Church and led to the draw-bridge at Fore Street.

OLD PLYMOUTH.—Stoke Church, and Gibbet (taken down 1827). From an old engraving. "J. Richards and W. Smith, for the murder of Mr. P. Smith, clerk in the Dockyard, in 1787, were executed and their bodies brought to Stoke, where they were gibbeted. Smith's body remained there about seven years and the other longer."—Jewitt's "History of Plymouth."

Where's Your Coupons?

A song that was sung in the war went, *If I had lots of coupons, I'd be a millionaire, Then I could live in comfort, and wouldn't have a care. Now I've got lots of money but that don't mean a thing. The things I want, well! I can't get, to rags I've got to cling. They are little bits of paper, that you can't cash at the bank, and without those bits of paper, then you've got no chance to swank.*

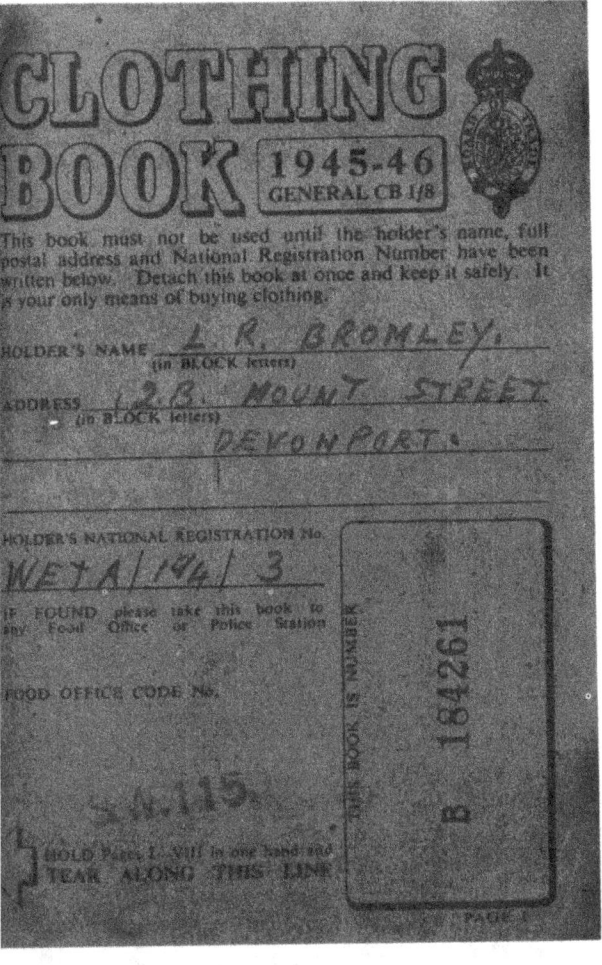

Civil Defence

Mr. L. Bromley was one of the many ordinary men and women who worked to safeguard life and property in the anxious days and nights of the war. The wail of the siren at night would send them out into the streets, blacked-out save for the searchlights crawling across the sky and the glow from the tracer bullets and occasional flares.

Air Raid Wardens relaxing, 1939

Mr. Harold Feabes, who lived in Gloucester Street, Devonport, is sitting on the extreme right. *Front row*. Others remembered are: Aubert Damerell, Miss Dorothy Hanning. They are seated in the Barne Park entrance to Central Park. The City was divided into six divisions each under a divisional warden. The whole area was again sub-divided into fifty-four groups each under a head warden. The city had a network of 135 Wardens' posts.

Guildhall Bazaar, 1920

The annual bazaar is being held. On the steps of Devonport Guildhall is the Le Marqu, Voss and Baldwin families. Inside the Guildhall were several valuable oil paintings including portraits of King Charles II, William III, Queen Anne, George II and Queen Caroline, George III and Queen Charlotte, William IV, Mary of Modena, wife of James II escaping to France by Opie, Queen Victoria, Prince Consort, Admiral Sir Edward Codrington, and Sir John St. Aubyn, Bart. Time was when magistrates held Petty and Quarter Sessions here, the meetings of the Municipal body being held in the Council Chamber.

Strolling 1920s Style

Mr. and Mrs. Yeo had a furniture shop near the Devonport Guildhall. It was situated on the corner of Duke Street and James Street. They are taking a stroll along Fore Street during the 1920s, they are pictured outside the Millbay Laundry which was approximately half-way between Tozers and the Electric Theatre. Their son Ernie became a vicar.

When St. Aubyn's Had a Pointed Steeple

St. Aubyn's Church, in Chapel Street, facing Market Street complete with pointed steeple is seen towards the centre of the picture. It was entered by a portico which was surmounted by the handsome octagonal spire. The Church of St. John the Baptist is on the extreme right. It was situated near the library in Duke Street. It had an elliptical gallery, the whole being capable of seating 1,500 persons. Raglan Barracks is on the right of St. Aubyn's Church.

Junior Technical School for Girls

This school was situated next door to (Saint Mary's) Reverend Bennett's Vicarage at 31, 32 and 33 Ker Street, near the Guildhall. At the rear were the tin garages of Mount Street. The school was bombed during the war. The girls had to pass an entrance examination at thirteen plus to enter the school. After twelve months they would go to Trade. Locals called it the "Trade School".

The Magnificent Seven

Back. John Hooper, Norman Crocker, Peter Hooper. *Front*. Jackie Evans, David Hooper, Malcolm Johnston, George Tucker. The seven are standing in St. Mary's Vicarage in Ker Street. Mrs. L. Hooper and her husband lived in the vicarage. One Sunday she remembers being blessed by the Archbishop of Canterbury, Michael Ramsey (during the mid 1960's). The following day, although her husband didn't want to go out, Mrs. Hooper insisted that they did. Upon returning they saw that the whole wall of the vicarage had collapsed. "Some blessing you had", was the comment of some people. "Well, it was a blessing" retorted Mrs. Hooper. "We could have been injured or killed had we not gone out".

Tape Measures will be Carried

Girls of Junior Technical School in 1928 wearing their sewing aprons. Some of them are: Cora Strewdly, Ethel Harding, Mrytle Homes, Winnie Clarke, Vera Jolley, Beryl Read, Mary Hyland, Hilda Bartlett, Ada Fry and Violet Rhodes, Violet Callsead and Winnie Mooney. The Headmistress was Miss G. Furnside, the tailoring teacher Mr. George Rickards and Miss Westlake was the senior dressmaking teacher. Mary Bickford (now Mrs. Bonning) went to the "Band of Hope" in the Ope about half-way down, towards Mount Street.

Ford Palladium

On Monday 5th August, 1912, the *Theatre Metropole*, having been closed for nearly three months for alterations, was re-opened with the new name *Palladium*. For many years the theatre had been known as the home of melodrama but with the invention of the Kinematograph the management decided the theatre should become a combined picture and music hall. Probably one of the oldest cinemas in the city, the building still stands in St. Levan Road. Over the proscenium were the arms of the borough of Devonport. It ceased being a cinema in about 1960.

Camels Head Cinema

The cinema, as a part of its operating machinery, had a large flywheel. Mr. T. H. Reed, who now lives at Milehouse, remembers when a boy that the flywheel blew up. It deposited a shed into the creek. The cinema had its own electricity. The silent films were watched sitting on benches that served as seats. During the 1939–45 War, the building was a police station. It is now the "Star School of Dancing".

The State Cinema

There were just enough red bricks left to complete the cinema in St. Budeaux soon after the outbreak of World War Two. The manager in 1963 was Mr. P. T. Richards who entered the cinema business in 1939. The *State* is decorated for the 4th festival of films. *Jason and the Argonauts* is the cinema's choice for 1963. The public were asked to compare seven films to choose a winner. The United States troops passed near the cinema en route to their invasion embarkation point, in June, 1944.

Arthur L. Clamp – the man behind the books

Arthur Leslie Clamp was a man of boundless energy with a passion for helping others, particularly through his love of history. A printer by trade, he started his career in a printing company before moving his family from Exeter to Plymouth to teach at the Plymouth College of Art and Design, where he eventually became the Head of the Printing Department.

Arthur with his five children.

A Devoted Family Man

Despite his love of teaching, Arthur prioritised his family, always making it home by 5:30pm for tea. He and his wife, Rosemary, raised five children: Susan, Angela, Elizabeth, David, and Steven. Arthur would often combine his love of family and history by taking his children on Sunday walks, encouraging them to appreciate historical monuments by taking photos or making crayon rubbings of gravestones for his books. The family home at 203 Elburton Road was a hub of activity, with a large garden, featuring a two-storey fort and a makeshift swimming pool.

A Lifelong Learner and Adventurer

Arthur's thirst for knowledge extended beyond history to a deep curiosity about the world. He was passionate about exploring different cultures, traditions, and cuisines, often taking advantage of his long summer holidays as a teacher to travel to places like India, Russia, South America, the middle east and the USA, sometimes bringing one of his children along. This adventurous spirit even influenced his home life, as seen by the short-lived family tradition of steam-cooking vegetables after a trip to Iceland.

History is a prominent feature of family days out

Community and Philanthropic Spirit

His commitment to serving others was evident in his long-standing involvement with the Elburton Methodist Church. He was the Sunday School Superintendent for over 15 years and served as the editor of the wider church's monthly newsletter, "The Link," for a similar duration. After Rosemary's very sad passing, Arthur later remarried and, following a chance encounter with a professor from India, established a connection with a missionary school in Chennai. Together with his new wife, Christine, he co-founded a "Sponsor a Child's Education" program that continues to this day.

*Pictured left – The cover of 'The Link' complete
with hand drawn sketches of each church by Angela
Below right – Arthur Clamp promoting his latest book
Below left – Arthur at home with his first wife, Rosemary
Below centre – Arthur on holiday with his second wife,
Christine*

A Legacy of Learning and Positivity

Arthur's greatest passion was history, which he brought to life through tireless research, documentation, and the many books he authored. He was driven by a need to "never be stuck in a rut," constantly seeking new experiences, meeting new people, and expanding his knowledge. With a positive attitude and a great sense of humour, he was always ready to help others, leaving a lasting impact on his family and community. His children, Susan, Angela, Elizabeth, David, and Steven, remember him with love and gratitude.

David Clamp, 2025

A Legacy of Local History

Below is the story of how Arthur L Clamp began writing books, in his own words, drafted shortly before he passed away in 2001. I have only made minor alterations to this text, correcting grammatical errors that he did not survive to correct himself. When I first discovered this text, I was shocked to see my name mentioned. It seems that, unbeknownst to me, I shared my first PC with him. I suspect he used it during the day when I was at school, although I do have one memory of sitting with him and showing him how it worked. It has been a pleasure to pick up where he left off and see his books republished and redistributed, and to know that I was part of the story, even back then. It was also fascinating to discover that his pricing structure matches the way I have tried to price the books, with a third going to local sellers and the rest covering printing costs with a little left over for my expenses.

I am his eldest grandson, and it is a privilege to curate his legacy, which we are calling 'The Clamp Collection'. The very last line of the text originally reads "The following pages list all the titles." Sadly, that page is missing and we have no record of all the books he published and knowing that some of those were researched by other authors makes the process of finding them even harder. I look forward to one day completing the collection and seeing them all available again. And maybe, one day, I'll even start writing my own to add to the series. For now, here is his story in his own words.

Steven Gibson, 2025

Writing and Publishing Booklets on Local Topics and Areas

I started this interest in either 1968 or 1969 when living in Woodford. I had by these dates established the Department of Printing and I think I must have been looking for something different to do. The first titles were of A5 size proofed from type set at Clarke, Doble and Brendon, Ltd., Plymouth printers, and then made up into pages and printed at Sawtell and Neilson, Ltd., Totnes.

Then began a slow process of getting them out to shops, etc. which proved to be more time consuming and difficult than actually researching, writing and getting the books into print. However, I persisted and opened a business account with Barclays Bank on the Broadway. I was advised to give it a title so I called it "Westway Publications". There came along another problem, one of storage of paper and finished books which was solved when the family moved to Elburton in 1970.

I changed the printer to Penwell, Ltd., Callington, Cornwall, as he was then just setting up himself and his prices seemed very reasonable. I did not get any of the printers to make up the complete books. I hand folded the flat printed sheets, stitched the books on a small manual table stitcher and trimmed them in a small hand turned guillotine which I bought from someone in Penzance for £40. It was brought up in a van.

The trouble and time going to and fro to Callington was too much so I transferred the printing to PDS Printers, Prince Rock, Plymouth, and I have been with them ever since. Now they are at Plympton which is easy to reach and they fold the flat sheets which was turning out to be a long chore which only saved a small part of the printing costs.

All my first titles were written by myself. I took the photographs and developed them in the loft of the house, the type was set by now on a computer situated in the house at Elburton from which I had collected photographic lengths of text to cut up and law down as pages.

At some point I decided that I would do my own film processing of lith film so I bought a large second hand process camera from Kingsbridge and learnt through trial and error to make line negatives of the text and halftone negatives of the illustrations which proved more difficult than I anticipated. The main problem was trying to keep the developer in the large dish at the correct temperature as any change would affect the developing time. I replaced this old camera with a brand new one bought from Croydon, Surrey, costing £900. This has turned out to be a great asset cutting out an expensive part of the printer's costs and one crucial aspect of the work which I could control.

By the middle 1970s there were many outlets I had contacted in Plymouth, up to Dartmoor, Exeter, around to Torbay, Totnes, Dartmouth and the South Hams. The market for local books was much greater than I had first thought and through getting to know many local people undertaking research themselves had the chance to help and make up books for other people who had in most instances, got together a collection of photographs with some text in a rather muddled way. Through my experience in print I was able to shape up their work and get it into print and in every case I had to pay the printer and let the person have the royalties. In the majority of titles produced in this manner this was another way of producing titles and it did give some profit to my work. However, I must say that in a few cases I lost out by either the other person getting the numbers wrong, not returning any monies from stock I delivered or they thought that more of their books should have been sold.

The print run was usually 1,000 copies and from time to time I have had reprints of 250 copies. It took about ten years to clear the first print run so I always had large stocks in the garage, workshop, etc. The numbers sold during the early years was about 7,000 copies a year increasing to around 9,000 copies and for the whole of the enterprise about 500,000 have been sold. The booklets have become part of the local scene and many people collect them, shops regularly order copies and I go around certain areas month by month restocking or replacing titles as necessary.

During the past year or so I have started setting the text on a Packard Bell PC, something which I should have done some years back. I share it with Steven Gibson, my grandson. There appears to be no end to the market for local books, but I could not earn a regular income because of the long time it takes to sell stock.

However, now exceeding 100 titles made up mainly of A4 twenty-four page booklets, some folded guides, with selling prices set with a third going to the shop which is the trade custom, the original idea has been quite successful and could go on for ever.

Apart from monetary benefits, however spasmodically these might be, I have learnt a lot myself, met many interesting people and have become part of the local scene with requests to give talks and to advise people about getting into print.

Arthur L Clamp, 2001

Death of local historical author

'He was an incredible character who was just loved by everybody who knew him'

Friday, August 17, 2001 (PPI)

SEVEN

A WELL-loved Elburton author has died at the age of 68.

Arthur Clamp (pictured right), who was one of the West Country's most successful writers, died at St Luke's Hospice, Turnchapel, after losing his battle against cancer.

Tributes have been flooding in for a man who was known in the community as a prominent writer and outgoing person.

He produced more than 140 titles during his life, dealing with both fiction, fact and history, often discussing West Country topics that were close to his heart.

One of his most acclaimed books was *The Plymouth Blitz*, and he also won credit for *The Rise and Fall of the Bearings of Membland Hall*, set in Noss Mayo.

He achieved sales of between 7,000 and 9,000 books every year and it is estimated that he has sold over half a million books, covering the areas of Plymouth, Dartmoor, Exeter, Torbay and the South Hams.

Mr Clamp was born in Mitcham, Surrey, in 1932, and was the eldest of four children.

He moved to Devon in 1941 to avoid the London air-raids.

Mr Clamp trained as a printer in Exeter and also gained a teachers' certificate in 1959 from Garnet College in London.

Plymouth College of Art, however, was to prove to be Mr Clamp's working home for the following 32 years until 1991, when he retired as head of the printing department.

He had a great interest in travel and had visited the USA, Tanzania, China, Russia, Peru, as well as travelling across Europe, where he presented talks and slide shows on his experiences as a writer.

Mr Clamp was a member of Elburton Methodist Church for many years, superintendent of the Sunday school and editor of the church newsletter, as well as being involved in much charity work.

He was president of the Plymouth and District Field Club and an active member of the Elburton Residents' Association.

He enjoyed leading walks on Dartmoor and historical tours throughout the West Country.

Mr Clamp married his first wife, Rosemary, in 1956 and they had five children— Susan, Angela, Elizabeth, David and Steven – and she died in 1987. He also had 11 grandchildren.

He leaves a wife Christine, after remarrying in 1991, and her two children and three grandchildren.

'He was an incredible character who was just loved by everybody who knew him,' said his wife.

'He will be missed by his family, his friends, the people he worked with and just everybody who knew him through his books.'

More than 300 mourners attended his funeral at Elburton Methodist Church on Monday.

The attendance was a celebration of his life – he would have found that really special. It shows his vibrancy and love of people,' said Mrs Clamp.

Steven Clamp added that his father was 'a well respected and loved man, missed by a great many people throughout the South West and far beyond'.

Picture contributed

This newspaper article, published by the Evening Herald on 17th August 2001, forms a good record of his life. Just as he encourages us to learn more about local history, we encourage you to learn a little about him. For that reason, we have included these pages at the back of all the most recently republished books, in honour of his memory and recognition of his contribution to the community.